HAUS CURIOSITIES

Commons and Lords

About the Author

Emma Crewe is an anthropologist who has taught at the University of Sussex, SOAS (University of London), and the University of Hertfordshire's Business School. She has worked as a policy adviser, senior manager and a trustee within international NGOs and grant-makers working on technology, inequality, and child rights. Her ethnographic research focuses on organisations, especially NGOs and parliaments in the UK, Eastern Africa and South Asia. She has published widely, including: *Whose Development? An Ethnography of Aid* (with E. A. Harrison, Zed Press, 1998), *Lords of Parliament: rituals, manners and politics* (Manchester University Press, 2005), and *House of Commons: an anthropology of MPs at work* (Bloomsbury, 2015).

Emma Crewe

COMMONS AND LORDS

A short anthropology of Parliament

HAUS
CURIOSITIES

First published by Haus Publishing in 2015
70 Cadogan Place
London SW1X 9AH
www.hauspublishing.com

The right of the author to be identified as the author
of this work has been asserted in accordance with
the Copyright, Designs and Patents Act 1988

A CIP catalogue record for this book is
available from the British Library

Print ISBN: 978-1-910376-07-2
Ebook ISBN: 978-1-910376-27-0

Typeset in Garamond by MacGuru Ltd
info@macguru.org.uk

Printed in Spain

Contents

Parliamentary curiosities[1]

If an anthropologist from another world were let loose inside the Houses of Parliament what would she see? Once beyond security and into the fairy-tale neo-Gothic Palace of Westminster, she might gingerly make her way into the Lords, past soaring arches, sculpted dead kings sprouting from mouldings, painted historical tableaux on walls, and into the cathedral-like chamber. She might catch the venerable Earl Ferrers rising from a red bench saying:

> I see that the noble Lord takes great pride in his name. He really should not do so because the only reason that his predecessor was made Lord Henley was to ensure that my predecessor was executed.[2]

Henley responded dryly that at least his ancestor had ensured that Ferrers was hanged by a silken rope, a privilege of peerage. If she left the Upper House, noticing the abrupt change from red carpets to green, she might get a rude shock coming upon the Prime Minister shouting insults at the Leader of the Opposition in a much smaller, plainer House of Commons chamber, jammed with heckling middle-aged men and rather fewer women. She may linger and persuade these strange natives to explain what was going on in each end of the Palace. She would hear MPs complaining that peers are stuck in the past, out of touch and naïve about politics, while peers would regret MPs' bad manners, tribalism and lack of proper work experience.

When I did research in the Lords in the late 1990s, peers talked of MPs as badly behaved: 'that vicious tribe down the corridor. Now *they* are cannibals' or, 'If there is a difference between the Commons and the Lords, the former is like jungle warfare while the latter is like being parachuted into the desert. In both places, it is war.'[3] Peers saw their wit as razor-like while the MPs used sledgehammers. One Conservative peer elaborated on the differences:

> The Lords is a much less political place. When people make their maiden speech, everyone is nice about it. A sharp intake of breath is the same as a yah-boo 'there'. It is run on judgement of merit – people simply cannot bang on, and the spirit of the Lords is [about being] the 'enemy of dogma'. Party politics is the enemy of debate, it is considered a bit vulgar in this place. On the whole the standard of debate in the Lords is higher than the Commons. Having the Committee stage open to whole house means that you got a much wider, more logical expression of views. As a result the amendments that are accepted are logical. Or if not accepted, the government takes them into account during report stage.[4]

I began a study into the Commons ten years later in trepidation, remembering the critical picture painted by peers, and with an ingrained impression of rowdy and childish squabbles at Prime Minister's Question Time and TV clips of politicians attacking each other and defending their own. But as I spoke to MPs and their staff they emerged as less tribal and more polite than I expected. As time went on, I began to understand why the recent scholarly research on Parliament makes claims about a stronger institution in recent years, even a revival.[5]

When I interviewed MPs I found they can be just as disdainful towards peers. Peers' expertise is either mythical or 20 years out of date, especially according to left-inclined MPs, and when they pretend to be above politics, less partisan or independent-minded they are merely concealing their ideology. Critical MPs tell you that peers are elitist and out of touch with ordinary people. In this kind of talk there may be an element of one community rubbishing their neighbours, a pattern found worldwide by sociologists and anthropologists, but the hostility between Lords and MPs is also, of course, political too. MPs and peers are competing for power so disparaging talk is unsurprising. MPs' rhetoric about reforming the Lords to make it more democratic does not usually translate into action because an elected House of Lords would inevitably challenge MPs more vigorously.

What happens when you look really close up at politicians? Is it possible to compare the Lords and Commons without moral disapproval or sliding into a political agenda for or against reform? That is what I have tried to do. The job of the anthropologist is to begin with a sense of curiosity rather than to rush to moral and political judgement, and although one's prejudices and political desires can never be completely banished, in this pamphlet I try either to expose them or rein them in.

My research in Parliament consisted of anthropological fieldwork between 1998 and 2000 in the House of Lords and 2011 and 2013 in the House of Commons.[6] I formally interviewed 260 people – peers, MPs and those working with them[7] – and I chatted endlessly in corridors, cafes and functions with many more. I observed discussion in the chambers, in committees (both private and public), in meetings, and on the TV; I also read media reports, blogs and Twitter. I shadowed my own MP and compiled case studies on a candidate's selection, a by-election, seven constituencies (including 32 surgery meetings), the House of Lords Reform Act 1999 and the Children and Families Act 2014. The more controversy I found, the more I investigated.

Researching in your own country inevitably means making the familiar unfamiliar and the unfamiliar more familiar. In the Lords I wanted to get to the bottom of the institution's hierarchies, ethos and rituals. In the Commons I looked more narrowly at the nature of different MPs' work and how it is changing. I wrote meticulous ethnographies about each House, but in this pamphlet I will spare you the details.[8] Here, I'm specifically concerned with some surprising conclusions that arise when you contrast the two institutions:

- Why is party discipline easier in the Lords, and harder in the Commons, than observers might expect?
- Why do women relish the Lords and sometimes struggle in the Commons?
- How is the process of law-making widely misunderstood?

These curiosities imply that we need a different way of conceiving of politics as it is already, rather than as it should be. And I hope this might inspire more optimism and interest when engaging with our politicians.

Party discipline: the whips have no clothes

The first puzzle is this: at first glance party discipline in the two Houses makes no sense. The general view about the whips, once supported by scholarly rational-choice theorists, is that they forcefully bully or bribe party members into obedience and that politicians comply out of self-interest. Many contrast the iron-like grip of Commons whips with feeble whipping in the Lords; Daniel Greenberg, a former Parliamentary Counsel, or legal expert, expresses a widely held view:

> ... comparing the effectiveness of the Whipping regimes in the House of Commons and the House of Lords is like comparing the four-times winner of the all-Wales working-dog trials with the efforts of an untrained collie dog suddenly let loose in a field of sheep.[9]

Why then do the gentler whips in the House of Lords achieve unexpectedly high levels of obedience, while their Commons' equivalents deal with increasingly rebellious MPs, despite those MPs having so much more to gain and lose?

'Whip' is a word with many meanings: the instructions sent out by parties to members telling them when to attend and vote; the enforcers of those instructions; and the process of encouraging obedience. The explanation of whipping given by whips themselves begins with the premise that the public put a party or coalition into government on the basis of its manifesto, so Parliament should scrutinize and improve the government's plans but not impede them. Government should have its way – especially in the primary chamber of Parliament, the House of Commons.

The 'usual channels', that is the party managers, whips and their staff, are tasked with keeping this parliamentary show on the road by keeping each other selectively informed, making deals, and outwitting each other. They coax their members to support the party line, especially during voting and interviews with the media, or avoid rebellions by government backbench MPs by warning Ministers when their plans are intensely unpopular. For them, the party member who rebels by voting against the instructions of the whips is arrogant, whimsical and putting ego above party and national interests. By contrast, those who regularly rebel see the government as too powerful and think both Parliament and parliamentarians should stand up to it. Whether it is conscience, the local party or constituents which are the driving force, when an MP or peer rebels he or she usually talks about broader loyalties and disdain for the control freakery of whips and perhaps of the party leaders.

Whipping works differently in the two different houses. The unelected members of the Lords talk of themselves as the House of independent experts, applying reason and wisdom to the task of revising legislation. The majority of the 790 active peers belong to political parties (182 are cross-benchers with no party allegiance), but most will tell you that they can't be compelled to obey their whips.[10] All peers have a seat for life, and most have reached the pinnacle of their profession so lack career ambition, which means there are few threats or bribes at the whips' disposal. The government can be more easily defeated in the Lords, as no government has had a majority there since 1997. Until then the Conservatives were in the majority, but two years after Labour came into government they removed most of the hereditary peers (who were predominantly Conservative) and the two main parties have been more evenly balanced since. Between 1999 and 2010 the Liberal Democrats held the balance of power but when they joined the coalition government in 2010 the decisive vote passed to the crossbench peers.

Despite all this talk of independence, party peers are surprisingly obedient to their whip, loyal to colleagues on their own side and only 'independent' from the Commons. In comparison, the Commons is portrayed by journalists as the politically tribal House, where lobby fodder MPs are supposed to follow the whip blindly, but in the lower house discipline is weakening, especially for MPs when in government. Philip Cowley's work on divisions reveals that MPs have been becoming more rebellious each parliament since the 1950s (see the following graph). The Public Whip website counts the number of times peers and MPs vote against the majority of their party. Of current MPs, 154 (about a quarter) and 245 peers (roughly half the party-political peers) rebel more than the average for all parliamentarians.[11] So although the Lords contains around double the proportion of more-than-average dissenters, the puzzle is still why the politically appointed Lords vote with their party as much as they do. By considering each House in turn we can shine light upon the mysteries of whipping at both ends of the Palace.

% of divisions to see a government MP vote against the whip, 1945–2014

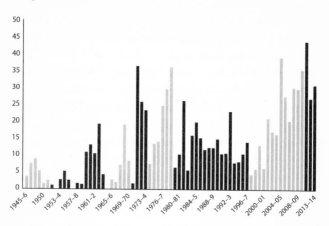

Source: Phil Cowley and Mark Stuart[12]

Obedience to party instructions in the Lords is achieved only partly by the whips. Three subtler social processes are also at play. First, the job of peers is politically simple – to revise legislation and scrutinise government – but socially all-encompassing. The Lords gets those who have risen to the top of their profession to attend through a process of seduction. Elevation to the peerage, stimulating conversation, the charm and comforts of the gilded end of the Palace, £300 a day for attendance and, above all, a sense of moral and political purpose, entice people through the magnificent Peers Entrance. They have not just become permanent members of an elite organisation but their names and identities are also transformed. They are humble towards the collective of which they are equal members and they share in its symbolic property.[13] Treated with deference in the House and establishment institutions, the peers enjoy an eminent social status, which seems to engender humility both towards the parties which put them there and to the other House. This is reinforced by constant reminders from old-hands that the primary chamber, the House of Commons, with its democratically elected members, should usually have its way.

This deference to others is taught to peers within the rituals of law-making and scrutiny. Peers have elected a Lord Speaker since 2006 but she does not select participants during debates. They regulate their own proceedings, with established peers encouraging restraint and punishing breaches with surprising ferocity. Impugning the character of another peer, or speaking at the wrong moment, can be met with angry shouts of 'Order! Order!' from all around the chamber. Party managers threaten even stricter rules if peers behave badly; the then government Chief Whip, Lord Carter typically warned that

> ... if even a small number of peers table Motions for debate without consultation or regard for other business, this House would quickly grind to a halt ... we would swiftly find ourselves having to tighten our rules and have to spell out more clearly what Members can and cannot do.[14]

So the rules and constant warnings remind peers that they are part of a collective (if an unequal one). The political philosopher Stephen Lukes has written that political rituals merely manufacture consent and consolidate existing power hierarchies, in this case the power of party leaders and ultimately the executive in both Houses.[15] Still, if this is the case in the Lords, it is not the whole story because rituals can be disrupted and occasionally they are, especially by those attending less often.[16]

Seduction and deference would not work so well without a third process: belonging. Belonging to political parties for life is a dying trend in the UK; the Caravan Club has more members than all the main political parties combined.[17] But, curiously, belonging has as much potency for politicians in the Lords as in the Commons. This is unsurprising for former MPs, of whom there are many in the Lords, especially as the MPs appointed as peers by party leaders tend to be those most loyal to party. But party loyalty stirs first-time politicians too. The late Earl Russell told the House what loyalty meant to him:

> My loyalty to my party is one of the strongest emotions that I possess. It is a greater loyalty to a collective group of people than I ever believed myself capable of. I agree – we all do – that all political effort is and must be a team effort. In my actions so far I have tried to give effect to that principle. I had been here 10 years before I voted against the party Whip.[18]

The assumption that the sustenance of political parties is simply shared ideology comes unstuck when you listen to people talk about loyalty. To vote against the whip in either House can feel like a betrayal of colleagues you have taken sides with for years. Or as one woman peer put it, when I asked about loyalty:

... it is not to Britain, not the abstract idea of the Labour party, or to beneficiaries, it is to party members – party people. It would be very difficult to be disloyal to party people. I can't bring myself to go into the division lobby with the enemy.[19]

To those who belong without reservation – those who talk about the moral turpitude of the other parties over tea, or help canvass on the streets of marginal constituencies together in the rain – voting in a different way from colleagues is an immoral act. The key sanction for peers voting against party – shame – is extremely effective. Still, some party members do not feel a strong belonging to their own side and might even regularly socialise with peers in other parties. Unsurprisingly it is these peers who find it easier to defy the whip.

In the Commons, whipping is different but only subtly so because belonging to parties can still be confounded by other loyalties. Even friendship gets in the way for whips. In 1979 the Labour government was facing a vote of no-confidence. On 28 March Jack Weatherill, the Tory Deputy Chief Whip, met his Labour counterpart, Walter Harrison, and told him, 'Walter, you are going to lose'.[20] The Tories had whips stationed in the bars and a spy in the local station of an MP who was too ill to travel, and this revealed to them that the Labour government would be one vote short. Harrison asked if his Tory rival would abide by their usual agreement and pair the sick MP with someone on the Conservative side. Jack replied, 'Unfortunately I do not have anyone who is ill. But since we do have such an agreement, I will personally stand out.' Harrison knew it would be the end of Weatherill's career and he chose to end his own instead. He owed his Tory counterpart for putting up with a Labour whip reneging on a deal some weeks before and, Weatherill added with feeling, 'honour among whips is precious'. Labour lost by one vote and the government fell.

Commons whips have more weapons than Lords whips. The 140 MPs on the government 'payroll vote' (with a paid or unpaid job in government) or on the Opposition front-benches (whips and ministerial 'shadows') have to vote with their party or lose their jobs. For the rest – the backbench-ers – obedience will be rewarded with the following: support if you get into trouble (which MPs seem to manage rather often), slips (permission to be absent for an important event like a football game or a play at your children's school), a good office, an overseas trip, or promotion to the frontbench. When the support of the government's backbenchers waver on an issue, the whips arrange a meeting with the relevant Minister and that often brings them around. But increasingly whips rely on pressure between MPs – most deem defiance of the whip to be arrogant or even morally suspect – because although whipping still constrains MPs, for a host of reasons whips are losing power.

The downgrading of Commons whips' weapons has been gradual over fifty years but has accelerated since 2010. Local constituency parties take less notice of central party managers, so whips' threats of de-selection sound hollow. They can warn MPs that their promotional prospects will be dented but examples to the contrary rather undermine their claims.[21] Stories about physical violence meted out are losing their deterrent power; it is no longer socially acceptable to squeeze someone's balls or shout verbal abuse to enforce their

obedience; backbenchers relish going straight to the newspapers or Twitter with tales of abuse by the whips. Whatever
is said about whips by backbenchers in public – whether
true, exaggerated or a bald lie – they can't reply: whips
never express their views publicly to the press or even in the
chamber. Violence only ever happened rarely but few whips
would now dare resort to it for fear of exposure as a thug in
the national press. A former Labour Chief Whip told me:

> Whipping has become hard because of indiscretion. You
> can take them to places where no one can see you ticking
> them off, but then they can tweet, 'The Chief Whip just
> said ...' Even in PLP [Parliamentary Labour Party] meet-
> ings people tweet what is being said.[22]

So Commons whips no longer use blackmail (much), violence or even angry rebukes; they are following in the foot-
steps of their Lords counterparts, acting not as bullies but as
intelligence agents, gathering information about backbench
opinion to avoid defeats, or as HR managers coaxing their
flock to stay in pens with no fences.

There was always an element of intelligence gathering. As
one former Chief Whip put it, even in the 1980s:

> Successful whipping is about anticipating the problems
> and heading them off or finding ways round them, or
> converting them, talking to people. It is only when you've
> made a mess of it and you've got it wrong that you might
> have to bully somebody to go and vote. The whole busi-
> ness is about collecting this information.[23]

It is for this reason that the greatest crime an MP can commit in her relations with her whip is to fail to warn them that they intend to vote against the party. But now the intelligence-gathering mode has almost entirely triumphed over bullying.

The person with the best intelligence is the Principal Private Secretary to the Chief Whip. The current incumbent, Roy Stone, formerly a civil servant in the Ministry of Defence, is only the fourth PPS since 1919. The PPS goes between the main parties to find out their plans for bills and take the temperature of their desires and frustrations. Party leaders keep their goals and tactics secret from other parties and even from their own members, especially since MPs have developed a habit of leaking to the press incontinently, but they reveal them to the PPS. He brokers solutions to seemingly intractable differences, mostly to get the business timetable agreed, never revealing political secrets to the wrong people. The whole process relies on trust, discretion and ambiguity. MPs told me that all four PPSs have been unsackable because they know all the secrets.

Whipping in the Commons is also becoming trickier for the whips for social reasons. They rely on party loyalty. Belonging to political parties is sustained by social relationships between members, which remain strong in the intimacy of the village-like House of Lords, but now MPs spend less time with each other than they used to. They all have offices with two or three members of staff, sometimes in distant outbuildings; they work fewer evenings in Westminster since the hours were shifted; and they visit their constituencies far more. The three current party leaders – David Cameron, Ed Miliband

and Nick Clegg, and recent Prime Ministers Blair and Brown – are not seen as particularly keen on Parliament. They spend less time wooing their members in the Tea Room than their predecessors. In 2013, when David Cameron was aiming to inspire loyalty after someone close to him was alleged to have called Conservative party activists 'mad, swivel-eyed loons', he did not write about abstract principles or ideology:

> I have met thousands and thousands of party members. We've pounded pavements together, canvassed together and sat in make-shift campaign headquarters together, from village halls to front rooms. We have been together through good times and bad. This is more than a working relationship; it is a deep and lasting friendship ... I would never have around me those who sneered or thought otherwise. We are a team, from the parish council to the local association to Parliament, and I never forget it.[24]

He wrote about social relationships. But email is no substitute for face-to-face conversation. As a US politician told the researcher Richard Fenno, no one will vote against you if you are on first-names terms, and if you chew their tobacco they will even fight for you.[25] Whether constituent or party member, people support each other in politics because they like and trust them, not only because they agree with them. One former whip told me:

> I would not stress loyalty to party or policy but to colleagues. If colleagues have worked hard, and then someone swans in with their prejudices, or what their wife says, or

votes against in a fit of pique, then I would not take kindly to it.[26]

Political parties in the Commons are becoming more fragmented not just because political and economic ideology is no longer as clearly polarised between right and left but because members criticise their leaders more publicly than they did in the past.

The more intense and frequent interaction with party members in constituencies draws MPs' attention more fiercely to their demands to vote in accordance with their wishes rather than those of the whips. For example, local Liberal Democrat party activists tend to be further to the left than the party leaders, especially in constituencies where the Labour party usually comes second. As MPs spend more and more time in constituencies, visiting at least once a fortnight in contrast to the annual trip that some made a century ago, they listen to local party members and constituents more often. If local party members or voters demand that their MP votes a certain way, it becomes more difficult to ignore them, especially in a marginal seat. Voting behaviour by MPs may not be entirely self-interested, but the possibility of either de-selection by the local party or being voted out by the electorate seems have a growing impact on how MPs behave in Westminster. Once, MPs might not have known much about their constituents' demands, but their weekly or fortnightly presence in the constituency, email and social media have made them far more accessible to each other.

Since 2010 whips have had even fewer bribes or threats at their disposal. They no longer choose Select-Committee members or chairs; the House elects them[27] thanks to reforms brought in to increase the power of the backbenchers. The Wright Committee reforms[28] also created a Backbench Business Committee, which allocates time to backbenchers to lead debates in the main chamber or the smaller Westminster Hall chamber. Their proposals must have the backing of MPs from more than one party and when Conservatives and Labour backbench leaders of the debates refer to each other as 'my Honourable Friend', usually strictly reserved for your own party, you know that the whips will face trouble. As backbenchers flex their muscles, and members on Select Committees grill Ministers and civil servants about government performance, we are witnessing a shift of power from executive (of which the government whips are a part) to Parliament as a collective. The coalition government (2010–15), and the prospect of coalitions in the future, intensify the challenges for government whips. An even larger proportion of laws and policies will be heartily disliked by a significant number of backbenchers in both Houses. So backbench rebellion in the Commons, and government defeats by the Opposition in the Lords, will be the order of the day for some years to come.

To give a flavour of the likely future for whipping in coalitions, consider the story of the Sensibles. In 2012 the coalition government proposed reform of the House of Lords. The bill provided that 80 per cent of peers would be elected by proportional representation for 15-year terms; few liked the idea, with the exception of Liberal Democrat MPs. Resistance to it relied on MPs; peers could look as if they were self-interested by rejecting change. So Conservative peers canvassed their colleagues in the Commons, and a mixture of new Conservative MPs – led by Jesse Norman, Nadhim Zahawi and Penny Mordaunt – and older-hands formed a group calling themselves the Sensibles. One had once been a whip so organised an informal whipping operation, dividing supporters into flocks of 10–12 who were in turn encouraged to talk to others. They informed Labour that even if they voted for the first stage of the Bill – so they could appear pro-reform to the public – they could help them defeat the Bill by refusing to agree what is called the programme motion. This determines how many days will be allocated to a bill; without it a bill can be talked out by any who dislike it. In July 2012 a Lib Dem former strategy director told the press that if the reform were defeated by Conservatives then the Lib Dems would retaliate by failing to support boundary changes. Since the proposed boundary changes were likely to deprive both Lib Dems and Labour of more seats than the Conservatives, suddenly everyone had an incentive to defeat this reform of the Lords.

The Sensibles continued their campaign on Twitter. Jesse Norman tweeted: 'any MP who says: "House of Lords reform is like a dose of the clap" deserves a follow',[29] encouraging tweeters to follow one of his supporters. When the Bill came to the Commons to be debated, few rose to support it. The final nail was hammered into the coffin by Malcolm Rifkind MP:

> The Bill is a puny measure ... if Christopher Columbus had been a Liberal Democrat, he probably would have been content with discovering the mid-Atlantic ... I have

not voted against my party on a three-line Whip for a very long time. I last did so in the 1970s. I do not know what effect it will have this time on my future ministerial career. All I can say is that the last time I did it ... two years later Margaret Thatcher appointed me to her Government. So my Right Hon. and Hon. Friends should be of good heart and vote as they believe, and that means voting against the Bill and against the programme motion.[30]

During the second day of debate Jesse Norman sent an email to potential rebels encouraging them to 'help the PM' by voting against the Bill. Through intelligence-gathering it became plain to the government whips that not only Labour but huge numbers of their own backbenchers were planning to vote against the programme motion. To avoid a humiliating defeat they did not even move it. Although the first phase, or Second Reading, of the Bill was passed it was only for show. The Bill was doomed. As a consequence, the Lib Dems voted against boundary reforms. Some speculated that the events were anticipated by Conservative whips, even if the scale of the rebellion and the venom towards Liberal Democrats were under-estimated. But in that case rumours that the PM raised his voice to Jesse Norman on the evening of the vote, telling him that he was not honourable, gave me pause for thought. Was this just for show? Then someone close to the action pointed out that by asking MPs to 'help the PM', Mr Norman implied that David Cameron was betraying his coalition partners, as Lords reform was part of the coalition agreement. He needed the Lib Dems to hold onto power so such a claim was a direct attack, whether unintentional or not, on his position as Prime Minister. Was Jesse Norman punished? He was voted Backbencher of the Year 2012 and put on the Conservative Policy Board in 2013.[31]

Obedience is surprisingly high in the Lords, and declining in the Commons, not because of the rewards or threats used by the whips in either case. It is the collegiate atmosphere in the Lords, and the fragmented, competitive culture of the Commons, which partly account for these patterns. Power is shifting towards Parliament in both Houses. Opposition peers and backbench MPs are growing in confidence, and both are defeating and constraining the government. Unveiling the mysteries of whipping exposes a complex operation of smoke and mirrors which depends on loyalty to your collective and your leader, rather than revealing a bunch of coercive bullies. As the position of parties and leaders weaken, Parliament's strength grows and government flounders even more than usual.

Women in Parliament: Performing patriarchy

Patriarchy in Parliament throws up the second puzzle. The apparent aristocratic social status of peers in the Lords might create the impression of rigid and old-fashioned hierarchy and, more specifically, patriarchy. In contrast, the apparently more modern Commons may conjure assumptions of equality and fairness between members. I certainly went into Parliament with these assumptions. But observation of everyday talk and relationships within the two Houses reveals the opposite: while the Lords have an egalitarian and co-operative ethos, and women thrive in the upper House, the competitive and aggressive Commons is a far less comfortable place for most women. How does this impact on women's participation?

Members of the House of Lords rush to tell you that a meritocracy reigns among peers. This life peer's explanation was typical:

> ... there is complete equality between peers. Working peers are not considered inferior, even former Senior Ministers are not looked up to. Dukes do not get more respect. Each peer is judged by their contribution, so internally it is a meritocracy.[32]

Earl Russell clarified more pithily that, 'peers rise as equals but how they sit is up to them': all will be listened to with respect in the chamber but the impression they make depends on how they perform their speeches.[33] In 1957 the first response of some to the idea of women peers was unfavourable. Earl Ferrers (the same one as we've already heard from) warned:

> It is generally accepted, for better or worse, that a man's judgment is generally more logical and less tempestuous than that of a woman. Why then should we encourage women to eat their way, like acid into metal, into positions of trust and responsibility which previously men have held? If we allow women in this House where will this emancipation end?[34]

By the time of my research, 40 years later, women were outperforming men according to nearly all peers I spoke to. Perhaps this is unsurprising as they are almost all life peers and have had to fight their way up male-dominated and often hostile organisations, whether the House of Commons or other workplaces. Memories of earlier hostility from male peers were brushed aside as no longer relevant by their female counterparts.

Women peers speak with confidence and authority, relishing the courtly style of Lords' debates where wit, self-deprecation and a light touch are prized above aggression. Women made up 25 per cent of the House in February 2015 but the only two peers attending Cabinet (but without full Cabinet rank) are women – Baroness Stowell of Beeston and Baroness Anelay of St Johns. A third of the 27 Lords Ministers were female, including the Leader of the House. In 2014 while only 20 per cent of government Ministers in the Commons were female, 30 per cent in the Lords were. The first two Lord Speakers have been female and the first, Baroness Hayman, noted that, 'it gives me some quiet satisfaction that should a man break through the glass ceiling to succeed me, he will be known as the first male Lord Speaker'.[35] Since the House of Lords Appointments Commission was established in 2000, 36 per cent of its appointed crossbench peers have been women. Women also seem to attend more often; the House of Lords reports that in recent sessions women peers attended 70 per cent of possible sitting days and men attended only 60 per cent.[36]

Nothing compels backbenchers in the Lords to be in the House, aside from peer pressure, so those with dependents or time-consuming responsibilities outside are less disadvantaged than in most public organisations. Barriers to participation for women are few; the only marked discrimination I could find was in explanations of failure. When male peers failed to impress it was attributed to their individual inadequacies whereas if women were seen as weak then their gender entered into the explanation. For example, dinosaurs (as old-fashioned parliamentarians are called) described two particular women being too long-winded, shrill and sounding like 'fishwives', and one Conservative male peer remarked to me about a female counterpart that, 'she is better horizontal than vertical'.[37] Although a minority of men are intensely disrespectful, they have minimal influence on the culture of the Lords and the odd demeaning remark from opponents does not put off many women.

In the House of Commons the situation is reversed. The male-to-female ratio of MPs has been moving towards equality but remains absurdly unrepresentative of the population at 78:22. In almost every site of work for MPs, women face difficulties.

1. *Exclusion in aggressive and competitive debates.*
   Although women MPs perform with confidence
   in deliberative debates, Select Committees and
   in constituencies, often they are not at ease in the
   most public rituals, the gladiatorial verbal battles
   such as Prime Minister's Question Time. Resisting
   the aggression is hard. One woman MP explained:

   > You have MPs banked up in front of you and
   > MPs banked up behind you, and when you
   > speak – for example, at Question Time – the
   > mass of noise can be overwhelming. If you
   > fail, then your side will leave with their heads
   > down.[38]

   So women may want to perform differently;
   they may feel inauthentic, but the pressure to
   conform to aggression can be irresistible.
   In informal meetings too, women MPs of all
   parties have observed that in a mixed-gender
   group where women are outnumbered (the norm
   in Westminster) various exclusion mechanisms
   come into play. A woman can make a point that
   is ignored but when repeated by a man gets the
   response, 'That is brilliant!'. MPs tend to refer
   to ideas voiced by male MPs, especially those

in more prominent positions, which reinforces the impression that they are the ones with the best ideas. Sarah Childs' research with women MPs supports the idea that the way they behave puts them at a disadvantage. In the adversarial world of politics, you have to promote yourself as an individual and self-promotion is considered appropriate behaviour for men while women tend to be socialised into diffidence. As Childs puts it 'acting in a feminised way within an institution characterised by masculinised modes of behaviour may limit one's effect'.[39]

2. *Time-consuming political party and constituency work.* As political parties decline in membership the shortage of volunteers means candidates have to spend ridiculous amounts of time in inflexible and anti-social ways in campaigning and winning support within the party as well as within constituencies. This is a serious disincentive to those women with dependents and no other significant source of income. In Parliament the sitting hours have become more family friendly but working hours for MPs get longer and longer each year, with the regularity of visits to constituencies requiring most to split their week between two homes during parliamentary terms. It can't be a coincidence that 45 per cent of men in Parliament have children while only 28 per cent of women do.[40] In 2010 the Independent Parliamentary Standards Authority, the new body that

administers MPs' expenses, reduced the finance
available for family members to travel between
their two homes. So time and financial pressure
may discourage women going into politics in the
first place and, once there, they report that coping
with family separation, running two homes and
caring for dependents creates pressure.

3. *Satisfying surgeries in constituencies.* I observed
gendered differences in the way that men and
women handle constituency work. All MPs do
policy work and canvassing in their constituencies.
But some men are less likely to do surgery
meetings. In contrast women are more likely to
describe this advocacy work for individuals and
families as the most satisfying part of their job. This
usually involves middle-class MPs representing the
interests of their often working-class constituents
to the state, either national or local. (Better-off
people employ lawyers or accountants.) This work
has value and women not only do it willingly but
often with consummate skill, using their abilities
to listen, show empathy and express sympathy.
Some men take this work seriously as well but
the only MPs I could find who rarely or never
attend surgeries seemed to be male. For those few,
their ambition was to get a job in government or
hold it to account; glorified social work, as it is
called by some, was a distraction. They delegate
this surgery work to caseworkers, who tend to
be young women. It is perhaps revealing that the

Labour MP Paul Flynn says of this relationship, 'The MP should be the living embodiment of the constituency, tirelessly promoting and defending the territory with the ferocity of a mother protecting her offspring.'[41] So are women MPs (and caseworkers) retreating to a less powerful, caring domain that sounds somewhat reminiscent of their caring role within families? Or are they showing the way ahead for all effective MPs? If we have more women in Parliament in the future, will more MPs dedicate a greater proportion of their time to this work? My personal view is that since these interactions ground MPs in the everyday realities of people's lives, and the impact of government policy and laws, this shift could be promising. Whatever my view, it is certainly worthy of debate.

4. *Misogyny in media work.* Lobby journalists, who are mainly men, are drawn to develop close working relationships with male MPs. They tend to refer to the male MPs as the cerebral, clever and promising ones, while women are subject to personal jibes and patronising assessments.[42] Whether female or male, hacks can be strangely obsessed with women's appearance. If women MPs are plain or badly dressed they are assumed to be bitter. If they are beautiful they must be dim, and if well-dressed they are seen as frivolous. When *Guardian* journalists (one man, one woman) rated members of the Treasury Select Committee for their performance at the inquiry into Barclays

fixing of interest rates, the men were given between 4/10 and 8/10, while two women were given 4/10, on the grounds that they were insufficiently chastening. However, one of them – the Tory MP Andrea Leadsom, a former banker – was focused, persistent and critical of the whole culture of the bank, and hit harder than some other members who scored higher.[43] If men are criticised, it tends to be their behavior not their capabilities that come under scrutiny: their drinking, affairs or greed, all of which play into a stereotype of dissolute male politicians.

The denigration of women MPs by journalists is tame compared to the misogyny directed at them on social media. The comments in cyberspace, where people hide behind easy anonymity, can be threatening and violent not only to the women themselves but those close to them. MPs reported that the negative press and related hurt and damage to their families was a major disincentive to staying in Parliament.[44]

The lingering assumption is that the norm for MPs is to be a white man; women, and especially black or working-class women, are treated as if they are space invaders, as Nirmal Puwar puts it.[45] The predominance of male MPs recreates this assumption as a reality. Something similar is true of people who give evidence to Parliament. During a period of two months in 2013, 75 per cent of witnesses to Commons committees were men, with only slightly more women in the Lords. In the category of 'experts', only 17 per cent were women.[46] Women are not the only group facing discrimination, although they may be the largest. Children, young adults, the elderly, the disabled, black and Asian people and various other minorities are undoubtedly under-represented as witnesses, despite efforts by the Select Committees.

Women parliamentarians face fewer constraints in the Lords than the Commons. Does this mean they represent the interests of other women more effectively? Scholarship on women's representation has moved on from the assumption that a critical mass of 30 per cent would automatically trigger better representation, although Childs and Krook point out that some stubbornly cling to this.[47] But feminists still ask whether women represent women's interests. What might be meant by this? If we are talking about *all* the females in the general population do they truly have shared interests? When you consider the social diversity among women – all experiencing life differently due to childhood experiences, class, sexuality, disability, race or occupation as well as their capacities as individuals – how can we generalize about their wants, needs or interests? Even my broad-brush statements about women MPs' experiences in Parliament do not easily translate into a plan for change when I consider the differences between women. Younger MPs told me that they were treated as if they were naïve, older ones struggle harder to get promotion as the party leaders get younger and younger and tend to surround themselves with people like them, working-class women face nastier denigration in the press, and those with dependents cope with horrendous pressure on their time and money.

Gender does not create stable identities that prescribe how women and men behave. Instead, as Judith Butler explains, the way people relate in a given locality creates expectations of women and men that are performed and judged. Your sexuality, race and age alter those expectations too. If we transgress expectations, we can face moral censure or even punishment, whereas if we perform our gender well then we reassure others that there is an apparent essentialism to gender roles.[48] But in reality within each cultural context the possibilities for gender and sexuality vary. A feminist agenda may be to challenge inequality and barriers facing women, but while we might fairly easily reach agreement about what these are in a given local culture – for example in the House of Lords or the House of Commons – the UK more broadly has multiple clashing and overlapping local cultures, so one feminist view of an ideal future becomes impossible beyond the abstract call for greater equality and justice.

Female MPs can't represent a fictitious universal category of 'women' as if those women are all similar and unchanging, or as if their needs will be uniform. So how can women (including those in Parliament) bring about change? Rorty suggests that feminists should shift away from reversing past injustices of a structural nature when aiming for change. Women's experience has been one of unrealised possibilities. So rather than women representing the interests of other women, as if shared interests could be identified, women can invent new identities for themselves; they can expand the space of possibility for other women through courageous and imaginative experimentation. Rorty writes that:

Only if somebody has a dream, and a voice to describe that dream, does what looked like nature begin to look like culture, what looked like fate begin to look like a moral abomination. For until then only the language of the oppressor is available, and most oppressors have had the wit to teach the oppressed a language in which the oppressed will sound crazy – even to themselves – if they describe themselves as oppressed. [49]

Whether women peers or MPs currently do this for women is open to debate. It was less possible in the Commons before 1997, when the number of women doubled and the culture changed. So numbers matter even if there is no magic formula. A new woman MP was told in the 1980s not to raise women's interests, or she would be marginalised for raising a 'minority' issue, but after 1997 it became easier, at least within her own Labour party. Structural change has to be the starting point but from there individuals play a role. In the Lords, Baroness Butler-Sloss creates the possibility for others that a woman can be a senior member of the judiciary and then an influential legislator, as I relate in the next section. Baronesses Hayman and D'Souza, the first two Lords' Speakers, both conjure a feminine and feisty way of leading ceremony. But women's institutional power also makes a difference: most women in Britain never see these characters; they are almost invisible. It is the women MPs who have the prominence in the media to reshape our sense of what is politically possible for women. Teresa May's toughness, despite the press obsession with her shoes, Natascha Engel's innovative and gentle leadership of backbenchers, Dame Anne Begg's calm and determined chairing of the Select Committee on Work and Pensions, and Jo Swinson's business-like approach to being a Minister and a mother: all show that women can be powerful without losing their woman-ness. They appear to remain authentically and confidently themselves while they run the powerful kingdoms of the Home Office, Backbench Business Committee, a Select Committee and a part of the Department of Business, Innovation and Skills respectively. Women peers may be equals to male peers but it is women MPs, and especially Ministers, who have the platform to recast patriarchy if they get sufficient support from allies inside and outside Parliament.

What might this mean in a practical way? When I gave oral evidence to the House of Commons Governance Select Committee in November 2014 I was pre-occupied with three aspects of my identity: appearing well-informed and independent, downplaying my anthropology, and being a woman.[50] All three played a part in my performance as a witness. MPs would not have taken my 'evidence' seriously unless I was seen as authoritative. While claims of knowledge and independence would fortify my position, I worried that anthropology might be misunderstood as frivolous. My gender may have made little difference to them, but I could not shrug off the feeling that as a woman I was an imposter in a man's world. I went into the Committee knowing it had been charged with inquiring into how the Commons should be managed. When the Clerk of the House and Chief Executive, Sir Robert Rogers (now Lord Lisvane), decided to resign, the Chair of the Commission (the Speaker) saw it as an opportunity to replace the Clerk with a general manager.

He wanted a moderniser (and preferably a woman) so he altered the job criteria from the last recruitment, with the agreement of the House of Commons Commission, so that detailed knowledge of procedure was less central. The Commission decided to appoint an Australian woman, Carol Mills, but when her boss in the Senate sent a letter deeming her to be unqualified[51], the Prime Minister held back from recommending her to the Queen. The Committee was asked to decide what the Commons should do next.

My view was that while most senior Clerks may be male, as in many professions, including that of politics, these Clerks are currently the people who know the procedure and politics of Parliament best. A generalist manager without this knowledge was likely to divert the attention of the institution's staff into the business of creating symbols of corporate professionalism – visions, long lists of impossible performance indicators and more elaborate risk registers – which I spend my time critiquing when I teach on the University of Hertfordshire's doctoral programme in management.[52]

I found myself in an odd situation. Despite a history of working on feminist causes in the UK and overseas for years, and generally challenging the status quo at every turn, I found myself protecting the existing management practices of mostly male senior Clerks in Parliament. It was less relevant that the top tier of management of the Commons is male – judging by the gender ratio of the new intakes Clerks could be more evenly split in 20 years time if efforts are made to ensure equal opportunities – as I was aiming to protect a gentle style of management, one that departs from the dominant forms of masculinity among MPs, so that both men and women running Parliament can be themselves. If I said this directly I would have been viewed as excessively academic or even crazy, as Rorty puts it, so, as is typical in a political performance, I used the rhetoric that would be most likely to persuade my audience. I tried to deal with the undertones of patriarchy in the House of Commons by emulating effective but feminine MPs, rather than pretending to be a man.

The Lords may be less male-dominated than the Commons, but it is the lower House that is more visible and has both the formal and informal power in the eyes of the nation. It is women MPs we are watching and since they can only open up possibilities for women if women grab those opportunities, we – women in all our diversity – owe it to those grappling with exhausting pressures in the competitive Commons, and to ourselves, to jump into the fray.

Parliamentary scrutiny: Reading the runes

The third puzzle emerges when you consider how law-making is understood. First, law-making is seen as either intensely political on the one hand, or evidence-based on the other, often with an assumption that the second is superior. I would argue that evidence and politics cannot be separated in this way. Second, Parliament is portrayed as weak and government as all-powerful, when in reality scrutiny by Parliament is becoming stronger.

Anthony King and Ivor Crewe are typical of politics scholars in describing such opposition and scrutiny as weak: 'there is at the heart of the British system a deficit of deliberation'.[53] And yet in the last 30 years both the Lords and Commons have intensified their scrutiny of policy, law and administration, and professionalised the way they are run. To give some examples, the strengthening of committees in the Commons in 1979, with the creation of committees scrutinising specific government departments, was seen as a way of checking government's power. The then Leader of the House of Commons, later Lord St John of Fawsley, explains:

> The principal reason why I was so keen, along with many other Members of Parliament, to introduce the comprehensive system of select committees was in order to seek to redress the balance between the House of Commons

and the Executive. I took the view that over the past century the balance had tilted away from the Legislature to the Executive.[54]

Thirty-five years later, the tide has turned the other way and observers need to catch up. Parliamentary scholars have confirmed that Select Committees are effective – a comprehensive UCL study found that government accepted 40 per cent of their recommendations and that, just as importantly, they generate fear.[55] Committees force government to account for its actions in greater depth than is possible in Question Time or statements in the chamber.

Since 2010 the members and chairs have been elected to Select Committees, rather than appointed by the whips, and they have grown in confidence. Committee reports regularly appear in the news. Since 2002 the Prime Minister has given evidence to the House of Commons Liaison Committee, composed of the chairs of all other Committees, for an hour and half once a term. The Speaker has allowed far more Urgent Questions; a handful per year was typical until John Bercow granted 40 in 2011 and continued at that pace for the rest of the 2010–2015 parliament. In 2010 the Commons established a Backbench Business Committee, providing opportunities for backbenchers to embarrass government. Some of the best debates in the 2010–2015 Parliament were led by backbenchers; they chose topics that government would have preferred to duck and they have even had an impact on policy.[56] They have often been charged with emotion; the debate on assisted dying, for example, reduced many to tears (including more than one on the floor of the House and me sitting in the

Visitors' Gallery). The changes since 2010 were a desperate response to the nightmare of the expenses scandal, which eviscerated MPs' reputation and seriously bruised their self-esteem. In 2008–9 *The Daily Telegraph* exposed several ridiculous expenses claims and a few criminal ones. It also revealed a broader culture of generosity with expenses to compensate for governments successively balking at pay increases, even when recommended by independent bodies, for fear of public disapproval. The body put in place to administer salaries and expenses – the Independent Parliamentary Standards Authority – makes all claims public and reports that not only do MPs avoid breaking the rules but that they under-claim. They subsidise the costs of running their constituency office because local newspapers will jump on any item that they deem unnecessary or amusing, such as shredders or toilet paper. Since 2009 the Commons has undergone what the Speaker has called a Dr Who-like regeneration.[57]

In the House of Lords a trajectory of increased confidence in scrutinising can be found, albeit for different reasons. Peers have long been proud of the quality of their debates in both the chamber and in Committees but were keenly aware that most of their work goes unnoticed by the public. It was only once the bulk of the hereditary peers were evicted in 1999 that they could wholeheartedly champion their institution. The Conservatives had previously enjoyed an overall majority, but only because so many hereditary peers sat on their benches which made them more hesitant about defeating a Labour government. But the House of Lords Reform Act 1999 removed this by abolishing automatic inherited rights to sit in the Lords. Hereditary privileges were seen as an anti-meritocratic way into Parliament by most peers and members of the public; once they were largely removed, the House of Lords was assumed by both peers and MPs to be more legitimate, according to Meg Russell and Maria Scaria, and it has defeated the government more readily.[58] Even the Salisbury Convention, which states the Lords will not reject a bill when passed by the Commons at Second or Third Reading if the policy has been placed before the electorate in a general-election manifesto, has been questioned. The opposition Chief Whip, and former MP, Lord Cope expressed the view of many peers in 2006:

> we now live in a different era with a different House of Lords. There has been plenty of argument about how the convention applies now, if at all. The House then had a built-in Conservative majority; now no party has a majority. It was then entirely hereditary, but since then life peers have been introduced by the Conservatives and most of the hereditaries have been kicked out by Labour. It was then entirely male, but the Conservatives introduced female peers, both hereditary and for life ... When Salisbury/ Addison has been debated in recent years, there has not been unanimity about its relevance or applicability today.[59]

It seems we now have a parliamentary revival, with two Houses of Parliament getting stronger in relation to the executive – the Opposition defeating the government in one (Lords) and backbenchers embarrassing the government in the other (Commons) – without either the press or public paying much attention.

If you look more deeply into scrutiny by Parliament, even less visible but important processes are at work which back my argument that Parliament has become a more interesting place. A tale about legislative scrutiny by the Lords and Commons will illustrate how Parliament can scrutinise effectively but also how the key concept of 'evidence' is always entangled with politics. Indeed, it is one of the virtues of our political process that time and space are allowed for the contestation of evidence.

For almost two years I followed one clause about parenting – what became Section 11 – as it made its journey through the Houses of Parliament. The clause was a response to the fact that every year 350,000 children of separating parents end up with no contact with one of their parents, usually the father. Many of these fathers contact their MP, complaining that the judicial system is biased towards mothers. During the course of scrutiny the government made three changes to this 250-word clause as a result of comments from citizens, the recommendations of a Select Committee and a coalition of peers, MPs and civil society activists.

The coalition government proposed a clause with the heading 'Shared Parenting' to be put into the Children and Families Bill. This stated that courts should presume unless proved to the contrary that the involvement of both parents in children's lives will further children's welfare. Public consultation produced a majority of favourable responses. However, various children's charities, representatives and family lawyers were alarmed. The Children's Commissioner, Maggie Atkinson, reported that children did not want to be used as weapons in battles between parents. Would this clause inflame conflict, many asked? Worse, should both parents be significantly involved even if children were at risk of violence? So in the draft clause the government strengthened the child-protection element. A commitment to parental involvement if 'not adverse to the child's safety' became if not 'at risk of suffering harm'. That was the first change following scrutiny.

The second adjustment was influenced by the Justice Select Committee. The Committee was considering the family-justice part of the Bill in a process of pre-legislative scrutiny, which is becoming more common. Witnesses spoke for and against the clause. Once staff had summarised the complex strands of evidence in a draft report, members debated it and in the face of slight disagreement, made the compromises necessary to reach consensus.[60] Their conclusion was that they did not agree with having a clause at all but if it had to be there then the heading should be changed from 'Sharing Parenting' to 'Parental Involvement'. When government finally published the Bill they included this recommendation as part of what had become Clause 11, even adding 'Welfare of the Child', to stress that this change was aimed to be in the interests of children not fathers.

The third change to the clause was the result of an alliance between MPs, peers and civil society. An NGO consortium composed of lawyers' associations, children's charities, family organisations and academics was worried by the clause. (Their reaction was that the clause was not as bad as the reports in the press, with newspaper articles, blogs and even a TV programme falsely claiming that separated fathers were gaining a new right to half of their children's time[61].) The convenors of the NGO consortium – Coram Children's Legal

Centre – drafted an amendment and sent it to the Opposition frontbench team working on the Bill.[62] It was rejected at the Commons committee stage as expected. So when the Bill reached the Lords the NGO consortium sent out a two-page briefing to the 100 most sympathetic peers. Chief among these was a peer with extensive judicial experience of child-custody disputes as President of the Family Division, Baroness Butler-Sloss. She met with other peers and the Coram Children's Legal Centre in a small Pugin-decorated room in an obscure corridor in the Lords. All parties agreed that it was better if the amendment was fronted by a cross-bencher. Who better than Baroness Butler-Sloss, with her iconic status as a giant of family law, with the backing of former Children's Minister, Baroness Hughes of Stretford? Baroness Butler-Sloss introduced her amendment in the chamber by expressing regret that Clause 11 contained a 'presumption'. Behind this mild rebuke was the terrifying possibility (for government and its supporters) that she might attack the whole clause. But, she went on, she was only providing clarity with an explanation of 'parental involvement'. She won by four votes.

So the government accepted three changes to the clause. No one could doubt that this Bill was thoroughly considered both in Parliament but also in thousands of discussions outside Parliament. People chewed over its contents, reading the runes or imagining what impact this clause might have on the courts, parents and children. On a superficial glance at Bill documents, the Clause 11 changes could have looked like the influence of one Committee and a crossbench peer, but it was really a process of far greater complexity involving conflicts of interests, contested evidence and networks of relationships.

Final version of Section 11 in the Act

The changes are underlined.

<u>Welfare of the child: parental involvement</u>

(1) Section 1 of the Children Act 1989 (welfare of the child) is amended as follows:

(2) After subsection (2) insert –

"(2A) A court, in the circumstances mentioned in subsection (4)(a) or (7), is as respects each parent within subsection (6)(a) to presume, unless the contrary is shown, that involvement of that parent in the life of the child concerned will further the child's welfare."

"<u>(2B) In subsection (2A) "involvement" means involvement of some kind, either direct or indirect, but not any particular division of a child's time.</u>"

(3) After subsection (5) insert:

"(6) In subsection (2A) "parent" means parent of the child concerned; and, for the purposes of that subsection, a parent of the child concerned –

(a) is within this paragraph if that parent can be involved in the child's life in a way that does not put the child at risk of suffering harm; and

(b) is to be treated as being within paragraph (a) unless there is some evidence before the court in the particular proceedings to suggest that involvement of that parent in the child's life would put the child at risk of suffering harm whatever the form of the involvement.

The circumstances referred to are that the court is considering whether to make an order under Section 4(1)(c) or (2A) or 4ZA(1)(c) or (5) (parental responsibility of parent other than mother)."

The network of relationships between Ministers, other parliamentarians and civil servants was complicated enough. Other Ministers, and some vociferous backbench Conservatives, were pushing for the promotion of shared parenting. Since this clause was in the coalition agreement any amendments had to be approved by the whole Cabinet. Also, any Minister needs to avoid alienating his colleagues or they may plot to get have him replaced. The Children and Families Minister, Edward Timpson MP, also had to contend with the conflicting pressures from his department (Education), the Ministry of Justice, the judiciary, civil society and various groups of citizens – as well as the endless misreporting of government intentions in the media. Underlying all this, the interests of fathers, mothers and children were entangled and sometimes conflicting.[63] Mr Timpson told me that 'it is as much about tapping in to the human element as it is about getting into the nitty-gritty. It is a very human process, it's about relationships, not just texts.'[64]

If politics is about making judgements between competing interests, this was intensely political: any assumptions that this clause was unusually scrutinised because it wasn't political (and at times *party* political) would be misplaced. The scrutiny was detailed precisely because it was. Politics, far from being a nasty form of pollution as often portrayed, requires adversaries in order to work effectively. Chantal Mouffe points out that

A well-functioning democracy calls for a vibrant clash of democratic political positions ... Too much emphasis on consensus and the refusal of confrontation lead to apathy and disaffection with political participation ... We have to accept that every consensus exists as a temporary result of a provisional hegemony, as a stabilization of power, and that it always entails some form of exclusion.[65]

Illusions that this policy might be (or even could be) simply 'evidence-based', does not stand up to examination. The idea of 'evidence-based policy' can give an impression that expert opinion or research consists of incontrovertible facts that can be turned into solutions, irrespective of politics. But different disciplines, professions and interest groups produce truth, and therefore what they see as 'evidence', in different ways. The anthropologist Bruno Latour argues that scientists and lawyers produce truth differently.[66] Scientific knowledge consists of universal generalisations and it matters little how these are presented. By contrast, in the courts, form is vital, including obedience to rules, and the presentation of evidence – making clear whether it is fact or opinion – establishes legal truth only in specific contexts. Politicians flip between different types of evidence but what is clear is that 'evidence' is never in reality one body of uncontestable fact, so its source, type and context deserve more thorough discussion. The contestation and debate of evidence is a vitally important part of political process but it is exactly this aspect that the media ignores and the public hardly sees.

In an ideal world a government might have approached the question of parenting after separation differently. If we begin with the intention of helping children of separating parents, then the government should tackle those factors that research suggests most jeopardise their welfare: parental conflict, poverty, substance abuse and mental illness. Children might also have been thoroughly consulted; in fact the UK pledged to do this by signing the United Nations Convention on the Rights of the Child in 1989. But these would require financial investment at a time when the government was intent on cutting expenditure. In any case government was responding to the demands of constituents, the press and its own backbenchers to make courts appear fairer to fathers. Given that imperfect beginning, Parliament did what it is supposed to do: invite interested parties into political forums to hear their views, debate contested claims and truths, question and challenge government, and propose alternative views. Given that politics is always messy and compromising, and that reading the runes is an uncertain business, is our Parliament really as weak as often portrayed?

Seductive gilded village and addictive city of torture

Our three puzzles have been at least partially solved by looking at the differences between the cultures and purposes of the two Houses. Peers have clear and limited roles – the revision of legislation and scrutiny of the government – and work in an intimate and crowded end of the Palace of Westminster. Their work is collegiate in various ways. The whole House rather than the Speaker regulates proceedings, the so-called 'usual channels' decide on the business agenda through agreement as no party has a majority, and alliances across parties form easily on many issues. The close physical proximity of peers – who share offices, have few or no staff and are confined to a far smaller part of the Parliamentary Estate – ensures regular contact. Most peers are no longer ambitious and they have no need to seek election, so co-operation between them is easily achieved. Their relative lack of political power is compensated by elevated social status and the charms of working in this political village. A man who has sat in both Houses, Lord Cranborne, now the Marquess of Salisbury, has described the House of Lords as a gilded village, while the House of Commons is a manic town.[67]

MPs struggle within that frantic and fragmented town. They are connected to the rest of society in a variety of ways and juggle multiple functions that can pull them in different directions. One particularly assiduous MP said it felt like Genghis Khan's preferred form of torture – having a horse tied to each of your limbs and commanded to pull. MPs inhabit separate offices, compete for promotion and places on committees, and engage in ideological warfare both between and within parties. A surprising number of MPs describe the loneliness of the job. One government whip pointed out that the whips are the only collegiate group in the Commons. Another said that the competition is intense. He compared Parliament to Smithfield meat market: 'You have two lines – let's say one selling lamb and the other selling beef – and the lines are in competition for customers but so are the sellers in each line.'[68] MPs are all trying to get noticed as individuals.

Part of the competition between MPs is about winning support from each other and everyone they come across. While I was interviewing a Clerk in Portcullis House café a prominent Conservative MP walked up to us and started joking with the Clerk, pretending to treat him as if he was unstable.[69] They had been on an overseas committee trip together so knew each other well. The Clerk kept trying to intervene and finally managed to say: 'Do you know Dr Crewe from the University of London, who is doing an academic study of MPs?' The MP appeared visibly shocked and in a second shape-shifted from jovial, chatty mate leaning over our table into an upright, straight-backed, highly dignified important person showing respect to an academic – an outsider – with formality, politeness and reserve. In a blink his face was transformed from twinkling to sombre. Successful MPs can adapt to different social situations without even thinking about it.[70] While canvassing, politicians do this every time a potential voter opens his or her door. It was only when I joined the three main parties to campaign during the Eastleigh by-election that I understood why politics can be addictive. Whether I was walking in the rain with Labour MPs, relaxed because they knew they would lose, and listening to their stories about the shenanigans of their whips; or recovering in a country club with Conservative Ministers explaining campaign tactics and worrying about the press; or marvelling at the Lib Dem industrial efficiency in their business-park warehouse, I felt guilty about helping because you get drawn into the intense competition, the performance and the camaraderie.

While the work of peers is simpler – they hold government to account and get junior government jobs – MPs have multiple roles and audiences. One minute canvassing door-to-door in a by-election, the next being interviewed by Nick Robinson on the BBC; on Monday morning listening to constituents in surgeries, that afternoon speaking in a Westminster debate; meeting civil-society groups, drafting a Private Members' Bill, contributing to the development of policy at party meetings, refuting accusations in the local paper – the chaotic list goes on and on. How on earth do they cope? Some don't. Alcohol consumption and divorce among MPs is relatively high.[71] But many do, judging by the skill with which they adapt their performances.

There are three threads that provide some continuity for MPs across all this chaotic diversity. The first are the riffs they develop to make sense of ideology and communicate their policies and arguments, each improvised for different audiences. The second are the rhythms that organise their work by creating repetition in time and space.[72] The third are the rituals – for example debates in parliamentary chambers, interviews in TV studios, and speeches at party conferences – which organise and punctuate the daily routines.

How do riffs, rhythms and rituals differ between the two Houses? Like jazz musicians, MPs and peers create riffs, as Chris Bryant (Labour MP) puts it, perhaps seven or eight at any one time. For example, at one point he had to mug up on pensions so he developed a 90-second linguistic riff, which could be improvised or extended to several different lengths. It is OK if people hear the same points in different contexts, but 'if you have a reputation for using formulas, then you are going nowhere', he adds.[73] Riffs can be useful for any occasion but your style and tempo need to change completely in the different sites because different relationships are being formed. So a good politician has riffs but has to appear as if she doesn't, otherwise she is acting impersonally. You have to be able to respond to an intervention in a highly personalised way to be considered a good performer. You need to have an awareness of specificity – the audience, the mood, the relationship – while also expressing a coherent view of your self and your ideology, which glosses over the fact that all human beings have ups and downs, and changes of heart.[74]

The popular view of MPs as locked in antagonistic and polarised battle, so necessary for a well-functioning democracy as Mouffe explains, underestimates disagreement within parties but also how much there are shared riffs between all parliamentarians that they tend to take for granted. Most obviously all MPs speak publicly about the need for action and change when trying to win support from the public.

Although traditionally Conservative ideas tended towards the protection of national institutions, since Margaret Thatcher's reforming zeal they have championed change almost as much as Labour. After austerity and cuts to state-funded institutions such as the NHS and the BBC, the Labour party, by contrast, is arguing for the protection of the national institutions that constitute the welfare state. In one sense Labour may be becoming more conservative, while many Conservatives are more impatient for sweeping reform of the EU, of immigration policy and of the way that the state provides services than they show publicly. So the two main parties are moving in different directions, but none praise British traditions unconditionally or spurn modernity. Modernity has become a taken-for-granted dominant riff for almost all politicians.[75] Even in the last 15 years championing traditions has become less fashionable in the Lords: in 1998 debates between peers often had a polarisation between traditionalism and modernity underlying them, but even peers are responding to the relentless pressure to appear modern.

While riffs give shape to the speech-interactions between politicians, their bodies have to navigate time (parliamentary calendar and seasons) and space (a vast estate in the Palace of Westminster, Parliamentary outbuildings and the streets of their constituencies in the case of MPs) by following routines and timetables or refusing to do so. These rhythms create continuity and disruption in their work, and their importance to MPs is revealed by the status of diary secretaries. Although some do it themselves, most MPs have a member of staff who arranges when, where and with whom they should place themselves, and patterns emerge when you look at MPs' diaries. Groups of MPs and peers can share some similar rhythms – mostly planned, such as attending a Select Committee, but others spontaneous, like sitting with your mates in the Tea Room. Other rhythms are idiosyncratic to each House (for example, visits to constituencies are only a feature of Commons work). Peers' rhythms are voluntary, self-created and less observed, so they can be more leisurely and less concerned with the appearance of frantic busy-ness. While peers' rhythms are simpler and focus on the Palace of Westminster (and departments if they are Ministers), MPs tend to have far more complex, rushed and changeable routines. Their every move is scrutinised by other MPs, constituents, journalists, tweeters, and even their staff. For MPs, even more than peers, the rhythms do nonetheless provide some continuity in social relationships, which makes it possible for them to have some continuous sense of self in relation to the world around them.

It is the rituals within the Lords and Commons that reveal most clearly the differences between the Houses. First, when does an event become a ritual? Rituals always have repeated performances, rigid rules, and involve the communication of symbolic meaning. In political rituals it is relationships between people – opposing, co-operative or hierarchical – that are the content of such communication. The meaning of ritual, and its symbolism, are not always easy to discern, as Kertzer explains: that the same symbol may be understood by different people in different ways is important for building solidarity in the absence of consensus. In fact, the uncertainty of meaning in symbols can be the source of their strength.[76] To give as an example, the State Opening of Parliament conveys different meanings for MPs and peers; this is hardly surprising, as it has to pull off the conjuring trick of demonstrating the majesty of the Monarch, the historical importance of peers and the political clout of MPs all in the same ceremony. The mighty procession from Buckingham Palace to Westminster, with its small show of military power, convey to all that the Monarchy is at the top of the status pyramid. The procession through the Royal Gallery, and the Queen placing herself in the Lords chamber surrounded by peers in their ermine robes, emphasises that peers are socially only just beneath the Monarch. Those peers who revere the historical take seriously the symbols that are paraded and which give the impression for a few hours of an unchanging moral universe. One peer told me in 1999 that

> All the protocols and procedures that reinforce the idea of the superiority of Parliament are important. During the State Opening there are many curious symbols carried about by odd-bods in fancy outfits that represent the enormous achievement of a settled government. To an outsider they may seem ludicrous, arcane and irrelevant: however these should be paraded from time to time just as reminders that they represent 600 years of stable government.[77]

The visible presence of history is seen as powerful in itself: to possess things from the past is to master time, and this mastery is a form of social power.[78] We have forgotten that State Opening was scarcely an event for much of the nineteenth century.

Contrast all this reverence with how MPs experience the ceremony. When the Queen sends Black Rod to fetch MPs by knocking three times on their door, his lukewarm reception in the Commons – having the door slammed in his face – is intended to indicate MPs' independence from the Crown. Dennis Skinner, a republican MP, customarily makes a small personal demonstration, such as replying to Black Rod's summons by shouting quips, such as 'Hey up, here comes Puss in Boots!', 'New Labour, New Black Rod', 'Jubilee Year, double-dip recession, what a start!' and by remaining seated in the chamber when the others make their way to the Lords. As they go, MPs amble, talking noisily and joking, making clear that though the Monarch may summon them with pomp, they obey only voluntarily and in their own time and manner. When they stand at the Bar of the Lords chamber listening to the Queen's speech they have the air of adults humouring children. The whole event is, in the eyes of most modernising MPs (and a few peers), faintly ridiculous but at least emphasises their independence and political superiority.

The scrutiny of bills and questions to Ministers are also ritualised in the two Houses and share some language. Both Houses have First and Second Readings, then Committee stage following by Report, and finally Third Reading. But they are handled differently at the two ends of the Palace. The policing of the rules, and the rules themselves, are the product of, and at the same time create, starkly contrasting cultures. Peers regulate themselves like a Quaker meeting, deciding when someone should speak, whether they have gone on too long and if they have infringed a rule or convention. At Question Time when peers compete to get in, the name of the preferred person is called out so it is the will of the House who decides which party and individual goes next. The rules are complex and depend on the type of debate; for example, some debates have a prepared list of speakers, whereas no notice is needed to intervene in a Committee stage. Peers consult the Clerks at the Table, if they can get to them, to ask for advice. Self-regulation relies on peer pressure so breaking rules can be terrifying, provoking howls of protest from all sides and shame and embarrassment for the speech-maker.

The Commons is regulated by the Speaker, a figure of great authority who is elected by the whole House, his or her three deputies and the Parliamentary Clerks, who prepare his or her brief and are on hand to give advice to all MPs. The Speaker polices behaviour; he or she ticks people off, hurries them up or metes out punishments, such as 'naming' an MP who has been rude in an unparliamentary way and forcing him or her to leave the chamber. Temporary banishment is extremely rare but the threat is effective. MPs, and especially those in government, prefer having a Presiding Officer to keep order and prevent filibustering. It makes sense in the intensely competitive Commons, but at the same time it casts MPs in the role of naughty schoolchildren, with accusations of Speaker's favourites inflaming rivalries and resentments. At the same time, Commons' debates are perhaps partly as lively and quick as they are because the Speaker or Deputy bring drama to the occasion.

In short, the social seductiveness of the House of Lords and the political addictiveness of the House of Commons are the product of, and reproduce, different cultures in each place. Culture is neither static nor outside people's everyday micro-interactions; it is continually created by participants. The self-regulated Lords is courtly and charming. It inspires surprising obedience to the party whip and is welcoming to women. The Commons is competitive, edgy and frenetic, surprisingly rebellious and unwelcoming to women. They can only be understood if looked at in detail and in relation to each other.

Both Houses are under-appreciated by journalists, pundits and the public. The veteran Liberal Sir Alan Beith MP warned that

> all Parliaments will always incur a great deal of public unpopularity, public dislike and public cynicism ... only when law and order is collapsing and democracy is denied do people start to see the merits of a Parliament ... looking for a good opinion poll rating for Parliament is not really how we should view this issue.[79]

Perhaps he is right in more than one sense. The inevitable messiness of representative politics, and the disappointment it brings, are both the virtue and weakness of Parliamentary democracy. When you take a close look at our parliament, and see how increasingly contradictory, dynamic and contested our politics is, Tocqueville's view of American democracy becomes persuasive in our context too:

> Its faults strike one at first approach, but its qualities are only discovered at length ... Democracy does not give the most skillful government to the people, but it does what the most skillful government is powerless to create; it spreads

a restive activity through the whole social body, a supera-
bundant force, an energy that never exists without it ... [it]
can bring forth marvels. These are its true advantages.'[80]

But political cynicism and even disinterest is not good for
democracy. Governments will always fail us, and be inclined
to hide these failings if possible, so Parliament plays a vital
role in ensuring accountability, and it relies on public engage-
ment. It is worth finding out what goes on inside our parliament and its direction of travel. Bagehot counsels that our
system may be curious but it will only work if we study it.[81]

In 2010–2015 I found that MPs are becoming less party
political; that backbench MPs – and particularly women
– are pouring more time into constituency work; that Select
Committees are gaining power at the expense of government:
and that scrutiny of law-making provides growing opportunities for opposition, contestation and debate. You can't
understand politicians' political tactics without looking at
their social relationships, and their relationships have specific
meanings within their particular local history and culture.
Any anthropologist would probably conclude that the social,
political and cultural – all with their continuities and breaks
with the past – are intimately entangled within Parliament
as they are in any other institution. Parliament is a barom-
eter of our nation's opinions and moods as well as a politically important fulcrum of the state. To understand how our
specific Parliament has survived in one form or another for
800 years on the once muddy Thorney Island by the Thames,
then look at the dynamism created by the endless shifts and
contradictions of democracy.

If the anthropologist from another world could watch the whole 800 years of Westminster Parliamentary history she would surely gasp at its adaptability, ambition and, above all, its resilience. She might be struck by the contrast between these two tribes – peers and MPs – in their adjacent settlements, mutually disdainful but linked by a few well-trodden paths. Lords, with their beautiful manners and thoughtful debates, act as if they are on a 'permanent farewell tour',[82] and are determined to embarrass government and protect the constitution. MPs compete in emotionally supercharged rows, perform a frenzied round of TV studios, promote their careers, causes and constituencies, and long to redesign society for the better. The House of Lords seems to be the happiest tribe alive while the House of Commons may be among the most unhappy. The biggest puzzle remaining for me is this: how could anyone find it dull?

Notes

1   Thanks to Peter Hennessy (Series Editor) and Barbara
Schwepcke at Haus Publishing for commissioning
this *Curiosity*; Richard Cracknell for guidance on
statistics; Phil Cowley and Mark Stuart for permission
to use their data; the Leverhulme Trust and the
Economic and Social Research Council for funding my
research in Parliament; Sir Michael Davies and Lord
Lisvane for the parliamentary passes and invaluable
guidance; the Justice Select Committee for allowing
me to watch private proceedings; and the following
for their comments on earlier drafts: Peter Hennessy,
Paul Coupar, Frances Butler, Nick Walker, Nicholas
Vester, Chloe Challender and Simon Patrick as well
as participants in a seminar at the anthropology
department in University College London. I dedicate
this pamphlet to my parents, Sally Ashburton and
Colin Crewe.

2   Earl Ferrers, *HL Debates*, 13 May 1999, col. 1345.
Unfortunately she would have to go back in time
because Earl Ferrers died in 2012.

3   In World War II, barbarous atrocities characterised
the jungle war in Asia, while the desert war in North
Africa, though equally hard-fought, was distinguished
by scrupulous decency on both sides. For details about

such attitudes, see Emma Crewe, *Lords of Parliament: Manners, rituals and politics* (Manchester University Press, 2005).

4   Conservative life peer interviewed by Emma Crewe in 1998.

5   See the work of Meg Russell, Matthew Flinders, and Phil Cowley.

6   I explain more about the anthropological method, contrasting it with a new-institutionalist approach, in this article: Emma Crewe, 'Ethnographic Research in Gendered Organizations: the Case of the Westminster Parliament', *Politics and Gender*, vol. 10, pp. 1–7, 2014.

7   This included 121 peers and 58 staff in the Lords, and 44 MPs, 24 former MPs (18 of these were in the peers' category), and 41 parliamentary staff, MPs' staff, civil servants, journalists and Special Advisers in the Commons or government departments.

8   Emma Crewe, *Lords of Parliament: Manners, rituals and politics* (Manchester University Press, 2005) and Emma Crewe, *House of Commons: An Anthropology of MPs at work* (Bloomsbury, 2015).

9   Daniel Greenberg, *Laying down the law: A discussion of the people, processes and problems that shape Acts of Parliament* (Sweet and Maxwell, 2011), p. 110.

10   This only includes peers who are eligible to sit and not those who have taken a leave of absence or been suspended. Membership of the House of Lords, http://www.parliament.uk/mps-lords-and-offices/lords/composition-of-the-lords/ [accessed 16 February 2015].

11   http://www.publicwhip.org.uk [accessed 4 February
      2015). These patterns are confirmed by the House
      of Lords Library, *House of Lords: Party and Group
      Strengths and Voting, LLN 2012/026*, 27 June 2012.

12   Rates of rebellion 1945–2014, http://revolts.
      co.uk/?p=711 [accessed 3 February 2015]. With the
      kind permission of Phil Cowley and Mark Stuart.

13   Emma Crewe, 'An Anthropology of the House of
      Lords: Socialization, relationships and rituals', *Journal
      of Legislative Studies*, vol. 16, no. 3, p. 316.

14   Lord Carter, *HL Debates*, 27 March 2001, cols 104–105.

15   Stephen Lukes, *Essays on Social Theory* (Macmillan,
      1977), pp. 68–9.

16   See Shirin Rai, 'Disruptive democracy: Analysing
      legislative protest', *Democratization*, Vol. 20, 2013, pp.
      385–91.

17   Conservative membership is down from nearly 3
      million in 1951 to under 180,000 in 2011, while Labour's
      decreased from 880,000 to under 200,000 during
      the same period. The Lib Dems have lost over 20,000
      of their 90,000 members since 1991. The Caravan
      Club has more members than all the political parties
      put together, at around one million (http://www.
      caravanclub.co.uk/membership/about-us/who-we-are/
      club-facts [accessed 16 February 2015]).

18   Earl Russell, *HL Debates*, 13 October 1998, col. 1324.

19   Interview with Emma Crewe in spring 2000.

20   Lord Weatherill told me this story on 26 June 2000.

21 Emma Crewe, *The House of Commons: An Anthropology of MPs at Work* (Bloomsbury, 2015), pp. 137, 143.

22 Interview with Emma Crewe on 17 December 2013.

23 Interview with Emma Crewe on 15 May 2000.

24 http://blogs.telegraph.co.uk/news/willheaven/100217916/david-camerons-personalmessage-to-tory-members-in-full [accessed 20 May 2013].

25 Richard Fenno, *Home Style: House Members in their Districts* (HarperCollins,1978) p. 56.

26 Interview with Emma Crewe on 24 July 2012.

27 To be more precise members are elected within parties and then approved by the Committee of Selection and then the House itself, whereas chairs are elected by the whole House.

28 The Reform of the House of Commons Committee was set up by Prime Minister Gordon Brown in 2009 to consider proposals to improve parliament. It was chaired by former MP Tony Wright so became known as the Wright Committee.

29 Jesse Norman, *tweet*, 06/07/2012 17:56.

30 Malcolm Rifkind MP, *HC Debates*, 9 July 2012, col. 52–3.

31 Nadhim Zahawi was on the same Board by 2014 and Penny Mordaunt was appointed as a Minister in the same year.

32 Interview with Emma Crewe on 1 July 1998.

33 Emma Crewe, *Lords of Parliament: Manners, rituals and politics* (Manchester University Press, 2005) p. 106.

34 Earl Ferrers, *HL Debates*, 3 December 1957, vol. CCVI, col. 709–10.

35 As quoted by Dorothy Hughes, *Women in the House of Lords*, House of Lords LLN 2014/008, 2014, p. 5.

36 Ibid, p. 17.

37 Emma Crewe, *Lords of Parliament: Manners, rituals and politics* (Manchester University Press, 2005) p. 118.

38 MP participant at a conference in Parliament, 28 October 2011.

39 Sarah Childs, 'A feminised style of politics? Women MPs in the House of Commons', *British Journal of Politics and International Relations*, vol. 6, 2004, p.10.

40 Rosie Campbell and Sarah Childs, 'Parents in Parliament: "Where's Mum?"', *Political Quarterly*, vol. 85, issue 4, pp. 487–492.

41 Paul Flynn, *How to be an MP* (Biteback Publishing, 2012), p. 138.

42 Emma Crewe, *House of Commons: An Anthropology of MPs at Work* (Bloomsbury, 2015), p. 173–4

43 Ibid, p. 174.

44 Ibid, pp. 174–5.

45 Nirmal Puwar, *Space Invaders: Race, Gender and Bodies Out of Place* (Berg, 2004).

46 The Democratic Audit, www.democraticaudit. com/?p=2278 [accessed 3 February 2015].

47 Sarah Childs and Mona Lena Krook, 'Critical Mass Theory and women's political representation', *Political Studies*, vol. 56, 2008, pp. 731, 734.

48 Butler, Judith, 1988. 'Performative Acts and Gender Constitution: An Essay in Phenomenology and Feminist Theory', *Theatre Journal* 40 (4), p. 528.

49 Richard Rorty, 1990, 'Feminism and Pragmatism', The Tanner Lectures on Human Values, University of Michigan, 7 December 1990. http://tannerlectures. utah.edu/_documents/a-to-z/r/rorty92.pdf [accessed 4 February 2015], p. 4.

50 Both the written and oral evidence can be found on the parliamentary website, http://data.parliament. uk/writtenevidence/committeeevidence.svc/ evidencedocument/house-of-commons-governance-committee/house-of-commons-governance/oral/15827. pdf [accessed 4 February 2015].

51 For a copy of the email from Rosemary Laing, the Clerk of the Australian Senate, see here: http://www. theguardian.com/world/2014/aug/18/australian-senate-officials-warning-to-house-of-commons-clerk-full-email [accessed 18 February 2015].

52 http://www.herts.ac.uk/research/ssahri/research-areas/business-management/masru/cmg/ doctor-of-management-dman-master-of-arts-ma-degrees-in-organisational-change [accessed 6 February 2015].

53 Anthony King and Ivor Crewe, *The Blunders of Our Governments* (OneWorld, 2013), p. 386.

54 House of Commons, Departmental Select Committees, *Research Paper 02/35*, 10 May 2002, p. 55.

55 Meg Russell and Meghan Benton, *Selective Influence: The Impact of the House of Commons Select Committees* (The Constitution Unit, 2011).

56 Emma Crewe, *House of Commons: An Anthropology of MPs at Work* (Bloomsbury, 2015), pp. 162–67.

57 http://www.hansardsociety.org.uk/wp-content/uploads/2013/11/Designing-a-Parliamentfor-the-21st-Century-Hansard-Society.pdf [accessed 4 December 2013].

58 As examples, Meg Russell and Maria Sciara, *The House of Lords in 2006: Negotiating a Stronger Second Chamber*, The UCL Constitution Unit, London, January 2007, http://www.ucl.ac.uk/constitution-unit/publications/tabs/unit-publications/140.pdf [accessed 5 February 2015] and Meg Russell, *The Contemporary House of Lords: Westminster Bicameralism Revived* (Oxford University Press, 2013).

59 Lord Cope, *HL Debates*, 25 April 2006, vol. 681, col. 75.

60 Inclusion of this account of Justice Committee private meetings is with the agreement of that committee, which hopes that it will further public understanding of the operation of the Select Committee system (3 September 2014).

61 Emma Crewe, *The House of Commons. An Anthropology of MPs at Work*, (Bloomsbury, 2015), pp. 192–3.

62 See their briefings for details: http://www.childrenslegalcentre.com/ index.php?page=

cooperative_parenting_response [accessed 14 October 2014].

63   For a summary of this see Emma Crewe, *House of Commons, An Anthropology of MPs at Work* (Bloomsbury, 2015), chapter 5.

64   Interviewed by Emma Crewe on 8 April 2014.

65   Chantel Mouffe, The Democratic Paradox (Verso, 2005), p.104.

66   Bruno Latour, *Making of Law. An Ethnography of the Conseil d'Estat* (Polity Press, 2010).

67   Interviewed by Emma Crewe on 23 February 1999.

68   Emma Crewe, *House of Commons: An Anthropology of MPs at Work* (Bloomsbury, 2015), p. 63.

69   Interviewed by Emma Crewe on 18 September 2012.

70   Emma Crewe, *House of Commons: An Anthropology of MPs at Work* (Bloomsbury, 2015), p. 223.

71   Alcohol Concern carried out a survey in 2013 and a quarter of the 150 MPs who responded believed that there is an unhealthy drinking culture in Parliament (Alcohol Concern 'MPs admit to unhealthy drinking culture in Parliament, new survey reveals', 17th May 2013, http://www.alcoholconcern.org.uk, [accessed 31 October 2013]). According to Conservative MP Charles Walker around a sixth of the 2010 intake of Conservative have divorced, separated or had long-term relationships break down by early 2013 (N. Hellen and J. Grimston, 'One in six new Tory MPs suffer family split', 3 February 2013, *The Sunday Times*).

72   Edensor, T. (2010) 'Introduction', in T. Edensor (ed.) *Geographies of Rhythm* (Ashgate, 2010), pp. 1–20.

73 Interview held by Emma Crewe on 25 January 2012.

74 Goffman, E., 'Social Life as Drama', in Charles Lemert and Ann Branaman, (eds.) *The Goffman Reader* (Blackwell, 1997).

75 Exceptions include Jacob Rees-Mogg MP. Emma Crewe, 'Westminster Parliamentarians: Performing Politics', in Shirin M. Rai and Rachel E. Johnson, (eds.) *Democracy in Practice: Ceremony and Ritual in Parliament* (Palgrave Macmillan, 2014), pp. 40–59.

76 David Kertzer, *Ritual, Politics and Power* (Yale University Press, 1988), p. 11.

77 Response to a questionnaire survey of peers about attitudes to the House of Lords, 1999. When talking of 600 years of stable government, perhaps my respondent is overlooking the Civil War of the 17th century.

78 Pierre Bourdieu, *Distinction* (Routledge, Kegan and Paul, 1979), pp. 71–2.

79 http://www.publications.parliament.uk/pa/cm201314/ cmselect/cmpolcon/82/82.pdf, p.38 [accessed 5 May 2014].

80 Alexis de Tocqueville, *Democracy in America* (University of Chicago Press ebook, 2000), pp. 252, 263.

81 Walter Bagehot as quoted by Peter Hennessy, *Distilling the Frenzy*, (Biteback Publishing, 2013), p. 134.

82 Lord Dubs, as quoted by Peter Hennessy, ibid, p. 144.